Sun, Moon, Earth, Stars

Overview

Poetry sets this theme in motion. Children will join together to read and create rhymes about the wonders of the universe and will explore new and familiar verses about day and night, the sun, the moon, and the stars. In the nonfiction reading, children will venture into the world around them and learn that their friend the sun is a star that helps everything on the earth grow. Reading Just for Fun will help children imagine that they are taking a field trip in their own classroom, where they will "visit" a planetarium, see pictures, and read about exciting NASA trips in space.

The language focus sections of this theme stress simple relationships and provide opportunities for children acquiring English to read and talk about themselves in time and space. They also include subject-verb agreement, rhyming words, descriptive adjectives, and opposites. Children will use language to compare and contrast, sequence, and visualize their place in the physical world. They will write poems and invitations and use symbols to record observations. Functional language topics in this theme include greeting people, describing weather conditions, calling for and getting help, and handling emergency situations. As children learn about the immense universe, they will expand the language skills that link them to the smaller worlds of their own lives, including their experiences at home and in the classroom.

Planning Ahead: The Theme Project

At the end of this theme, children will design a hands-on science center—a museum of their own. Plan to invite friends in mainstream classes and family members to visit the museum. Early in the theme, start collecting recycled materials that children can use to create museum displays about the sun, the moon, the earth, and the stars. As you work through the theme, facilitate learning by encouraging children to show one another their work and talk about their progress on the theme project.

Getting Ready to Read

What Do Children Know?

Invite children to share with you what they know about the sun, moon, earth, and stars. Use questions such as the following to assess children's prior knowledge and their ability to express it in English.

▶ *Where is up? Point up. Where is down. Point down.* (P)*

▶ *Is the sun up or down? Where is the earth?* (EP)*

▶ *What can you see up in the sky during the day? What can you see at night?* (SE)*

▶ *How is day different from night?* (NF)*

Tape two sheets of chart paper together and post them on the wall to use as compare-and-contrast charts. Write *Sky* at the top of the chart and *Earth* at the bottom. Draw a sun on one sheet. Ask, *Is it day or night?* Label it *day.* Draw a crescent moon on the other sheet and let children tell you to label it *night.* Next, invite children to tell what they see in the sky during the day and at night. Record their responses on the appropriate sheet. Invite children to contribute drawings, words, or invented writings to the charts.

What Do Children Want to Know?

Ask what they would like to know about the sun, moon, Earth, or stars. Make a list of their questions on another chart.

Theme Presentation

OBJECTIVES

● **READING** To activate prior knowledge and vocabulary
● **LISTENING/SPEAKING** To categorize information about day and night/To compare and contrast day and night
● **WRITING** To copy words

KEY VOCABULARY

day, night, morning, sun, moon, cloud, star, light, dark, awake, asleep, get up, go to bed

Introduce

▶ Ask children to look at page 2 or Transparency 1. Review the main words from the compare-and-contrast chart by asking individuals to point to or identify the items. For example: *Point to the moon. Show me a star. What's this?* Encourage children to repeat the words.

▶ Help them talk further about the picture by responding to questions, such as:

Raise your hand if this is a day picture. (PREPRODUCTION)
Is it morning or night? Is the boy asleep or awake? (EARLY PRODUCTION)
When does it get dark? (SPEECH EMERGENCE)
Describe what the boy is doing in the pictures. (NEARLY-FLUENT)

Practice

You may wish to reinforce children's understanding of this lesson by using Activity Page 1. (Be sure preproduction and early-production students understand the instructions.)

When children finish the activity page, invite them to work in small groups. Have one child pantomime an activity while the others guess if it's done *during the day* or *at night.* The child who guesses correctly pantomimes the next activity. Some children also may be able to name the activity. (This game can be adapted for the entire class.)

Evaluate

Use the activity page and pantomiming activity to evaluate informally. You may note the child's physical and oral responses on the back of Activity Page 1. This can be included in the child's portfolio as a point of entry to measure progress throughout the theme.

Hello, Day!

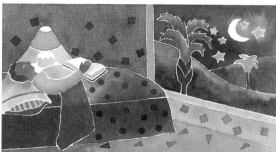

Hello, Night!

2 Sun, Moon, Earth, Stars

Preview • *I See the Moon; Day and Night; Twinkle, Twinkle*

OBJECTIVES

- **READING** To match written words with pictures/To use illustrations and titles to predict content
- **LISTENING/SPEAKING** To demonstrate understanding through movement

KEY VOCABULARY

sky, comes up, goes down, comes out, earth, world, spin, spinning, round, high

Read the words. Point to the picture that matches each word.

star	sun	earth	moon	sky

3

Vocabulary Preview

▶ Introduce new words and expressions by asking questions, such as:

Point to the sky. **(P)***
Does the sun or the moon come up in the morning? **(EP)***
Tell me what comes out at night. **(SE)***
How does the sun look on a cloudy day? **(NF)***

▶ Ask children to look at Transparency 2 or page 3. As you read the words at the bottom of the page, have them point to the corresponding objects in the picture. Invite volunteers to read the words. Have other children draw corresponding pictures on the board as you read the words aloud.

  ▶ Invite children to play a movement game. Tell them to listen to you and move the way the sun, moon, earth, and stars do. Play some appropriate "star" music and have children lie down and pretend to sleep. Use guided imagery, as follows: *You are the sun. You come up slowly and move higher and higher in the sky.* Have them be stars that twinkle their points (fingers), then be the moon that goes from big and round to very skinny; and finally be the earth that spins (sitting on the floor).

Looking Ahead

▦ Form three groups. Using three pupil books and stick-on notes, cover the text of a different poem in each book. Have each group use the title and illustration(s) to help them guess what the poem is about. Invite the groups to share their predictions.

*Language Acquisition Levels: P = PREPRODUCTION;
EP = EARLY PRODUCTION; SE = SPEECH EMERGENCE;
NF = NEARLY-FLUENT

HOME–SCHOOL CONNECTION

Send home Activity Page 2, which suggests that family members write out a poem, rhyme, or song from their home culture for the child to illustrate. You may wish to have this letter translated into languages not supplied by the publisher.

When Activity Page 2 is returned, ask each child to share his or her home-culture piece with the class. Invite children to create a bulletin board display or book of their work. You may want to classify pieces by the main topic, *Sun, Moon, Earth, Stars,* and to use home language words as subtitles. Help children gain an awareness of cultural similarities and differences that the pictures or rhymes may show.

Rereading for Different Purposes

▶ Invite children to listen to the poems on the audio tape. Encourage them to think about actions they might perform to pantomime the poems. Then play the tape again and ask children to add their movements.

▶ Encourage children to read or recite the poems chorally, with or without gestures. Some children may want to record an individual reading for their audio portfolio.

Reading the Literature

I See the Moon; Day and Night; Twinkle, Twinkle

Introduce

▶ Invite children to stand around a globe. Ask what the globe shows or represents. (*the earth, the world*) Spin the globe and encourage them to tell what you are doing. *(spinning the globe)* Ask children to spin like the globe, but slowly.

▶ Then use a flashlight to represent the sun and the globe to represent the earth to help children understand why we have day and night. Point out your location on the globe. You may wish to mark it with a wax pencil. Then darken the room, and ask a volunteer to hold the sun (flashlight) so that it shines on the side of the globe where you live. Help children understand that it is daytime where you live because your location is facing the sun. Then slowly turn the globe to show that as your location moves away from the sun, it gets dark and daytime turns to nighttime. Children may enjoy using the globe and flashlight to see whether it is day or night in their home countries when it is day where they live now.

▶ Invite children to say *good morning* or *good night* in English or in their home language as if they're greeting their family or friends while you spin the globe.

Read

▶ On the first reading from the Big Book, allow children to enjoy the rhyme and rhythm of the poetry, without interruption for questions, explanations, or language focus points.

▶ To help children identify the rhythm, scan the poem by clapping or tapping its meter. Invite children to do likewise as you repeat the poem.

On These Pages

Call students' attention to the words *I* and *me*. Discuss the idea that both words refer to the same person.

LITERATURE PART 1 FICTION

I See the Moon

I see the moon,
and the moon sees me.
I like the moon,
and the moon likes me.

4   Sun, Moon, Earth, Stars

Meeting Individual Needs

REINFORCEMENT

▶ Since some children learn best through music, you may wish to play the songs "I See the Moon" and "Twinkle, Twinkle" from the audio tape. Play the songs several times and encourage children to join in. Then invite children to play rhythm instruments as they listen to the songs. You may wish to have children take turns playing instruments while the other children sing.

▶ *Spatial* and *kinesthetic* learners may enjoy contributing to a classroom galaxy. You may wish to have these children make a collage of day and nighttime skies. Provide finger paints and construction paper for making the background. Children might use aluminum foil for stars and tissue paper or cotton balls for clouds. Invite children to work alone or in small groups. Encourage them to label their work or dictate labels for you to record.

BUILDING SELF-ESTEEM

Celebrate the "student stars" in your classroom. Provide children with star patterns and tag board. Ask each child to trace the pattern and cut out a tag board star. Invite children to cover their stars with aluminum foil. Paste each child's picture and name on a star and hang them from the ceiling. (You may want to use pictures taken with self-developing cameras or self-drawn student portraits.)

CHALLENGE

Invite children to choose books from the library or class collection that deal with the sun, moon, earth, and stars. More fluent readers may read aloud or retell the books. Nonreaders may name things they see on the pages or invent stories to go with the pictures, depending on their level of proficiency.

Story Card 1

Cross-Curricular Connections

HEALTH

You may wish to use a chart to help students keep a log of healthful things they do during the day and at night. (Examples: brush teeth, eat apples, get enough sleep) You may need to brainstorm the kinds of things that are necessary to stay strong and healthy every day.

ART/MULTICULTURAL

Tell children that many people in different cultures tell stories about the sun, moon, and stars. Explain that some Native Americans believed that the sun and the moon were brother and sister. To help children think about this idea, you may wish to stimulate a discussion by asking questions such as the following: *Why do you think they thought the sun and moon were brother and sister? Who do you think was the brother? Who do you think was the sister? Why?*
Then provide children with drawing paper and invite them to draw a picture of the sun and the moon as brother and sister.

MATH

Invite children to name and point out the shapes they see in the pictures on page 2. Make labels (*circle, square, triangle*) on index cards and place them on the chalkboard ledge. Have children work in groups to count each shape. Then stack up blocks under the appropriate headings to make a bar graph.

MUSIC/MOVEMENT

Each of the poems lends itself to simple musical and rhythmic accompaniment. Invite children to use gongs, drums, blocks, triangles, and a xylophone to create musical backgrounds for a reading of the poems. Record the musical compositions. Then encourage children to express themselves through creative movement. First have them move in silence with your verbal direction. For example: *It's night. You are each a star. Let me see you move through the sky. Now spin slowly round and round. Now stop spinning and show me the points on your star. Make your star twinkle.* Next, play the recording and let the children create their own movements to the words and music.

Mainstream Connections

Invite mainstream students to a recital of the poems and movement studies the children have created. At the end of the program, invite the visitors to join the class in a creative movement activity about the sky and the earth.

The sun comes up.
The moon goes down.
The earth keeps spinning,
round and round.

6   Sun, Moon, Earth, Stars

On These Pages

Use different-sized pieces of clay to represent the sun, moon, and Earth. Using these pieces, demonstrate how the earth moves around the sun, and the moon moves around the earth. Invite volunteers to take turns moving the pieces, stopping at times to point out which side of the "earth" is facing the sun and therefore has light or daytime. To help children visualize the relationship between the earth, the sun, and the moon, cut out a large yellow circle for the sun, a large blue circle for the earth, and a smaller white circle for the moon. Write the words *sun, earth,* and *moon* on the appropriate circles.

Language Focus

● **Subject-verb agreement**

▶ Help children understand that in English we use different action words depending on who is doing something. Write the first two lines of *I See the Moon* on the board. Read the sentences aloud. Point out that in the first sentence, we use the action word *see* because the person *I* is doing the action. In the second sentence, we use *sees* because *the moon* is doing something.

▶ Invite children to look at *Day and Night*. Read the poem aloud. Encourage children to substitute *I* for the words *the moon*, *the sun*, and *the earth*. Remind them that they will need to use a different action word because the person doing the action

changed. Repeat verses using *we*, *you*, and the names of individual students.

Theme Project Update

To help children recall some of the information they have learned, you may invite them to walk around the classroom and look at all the writings, drawings, charts, and graphs. Encourage children to think about how they might use these items and others in the room for their class science museum.

▶ This might be a good time to share museum brochures with children. Describe a visit you took to a museum, what you saw, and how you felt about it. If possible, take children on a trip to a museum or planetarium.

Everyday Talk

● **Greeting someone**

Invite children to brainstorm different ways to greet people throughout the day. Make a list by time of day: **Morning**—*good morning*; **Afternoon**—*good afternoon*; **Night**—*good evening* (Point out that *good night* is only used to say good-bye or when you go to bed.); **Anytime**—*hello, hi*. Have students form two circles. Ask them to walk in opposite directions, stop, and greet each person as you tell the time of day. *(in the morning, after school, etc.)*

The moon comes up.
The sun goes down.
The earth still spins,
without a sound.

7

What Did Children Learn?

Invite children to look at the compare-and-contrast charts they started before reading the poems. Talk about the entries on the charts. Encourage children to add anything new they learned from the poems. Discuss the fact that these poems helped them learn about the sun, moon, Earth, and stars. You may wish to expand the chart to include day-time and nighttime activities.

WRITER'S JOURNAL

Invite the children to think about their favorite time of day. Suggest they describe that time and talk or draw about something they like to do then.

After You Read

Post-Reading Activities

Vocabulary Check

Write key words from the theme vocabulary and poems on paper stars, one word per star. Place stars in a bag. Children take turns pulling out a star. Ask the child to read the word aloud and show or tell the word's meaning.

Comprehension Check

▶ Have children complete the matching activity on page 9. While more proficient readers work independently, help nonreaders and less fluent children complete the activity. Have all come together to discuss the activity and allow the readers to check their work.

▶ Introduce and accompany the following rhyme with syncopated movement.

Hello, Day! Hello, Day! [wave]/*I'm waking up to see you today.* [stand up, rub eyes, stretch]/*Then I'm off to school* [walk]/*To work and play.* [write or open book, toss ball or jump rope]

Next, recite: *Hello, Night! Hello, Night!/The stars are bright./I'm lying down in bed,/Tucked in tight.*

Repeat the rhyme and accompany it with a finger play or pantomime. Play the tape and have children join in. Then play the audio tape and have children parade around in a circle as they listen. Invite them to add new gestures to the words.

Practice

Write two sets of sentences (one for pre-production and early-production students and one for speech-emergent and nearly-fluent students) on sheets of paper that can be cut into strips with one sentence on each. Have less fluent students say *day* or *night* for each sentence, such as: *The sky is blue. The stars come out. It's time to go to bed.* Give more fluent students sentences requiring a fill-in, such as: *The _____ goes down at night. The star twinkles like a _____. The earth keeps _____ round and round.* Divide the class into 3 or 4 groups of children of mixed proficiency levels. Put the sentence strips into two boxes according to level of difficulty. Have each child draw one strip from the appropriate box and answer the question. If the answer is correct, the child can keep the question. If the answer is incorrect, the slip goes back into the box.

On These Pages

▶ *Wonder* may be difficult for children. Explain it as "to think but not know, to be uncertain, to be curious, to doubt."

▶ To demonstrate the meaning of *twinkle* and *diamond,* hang twinkle lights overhead. Show children some diamond or rhinestone jewelry to help them understand how stars are like diamonds. Check how many other words children know to describe the light from the stars, sun, and moon. (*shine, glow, sparkle*)

▶ Provide each child with a 9-by-11-inch construction paper frame, a copy of one of the poems, and a selection of magazines, greeting cards, and stickers. Encourage children to cut out pictures to represent their poems. Help children paste their poems in the frames. When they are finished, invite children to recite, retell, or dramatize their poems. Children can then use these framed poems as gifts for their mainstream friends or for a family member.

▶ Children may also enjoy creating new illustrations for the poems. Encourage

Twinkle, twinkle, little star,
how I wonder what you are!
Up above the world so high,
like a diamond in the sky.

8 Sun, Moon, Earth, Stars

each child to illustrate the poem of his or her choice. Display the finished illustrations around the poems.

Language Focus

● **Rhyming words**

▶ Tell children that when words have the same ending sound, the words rhyme. (*moon, spoon; sun, fun*) Read the first line of "Twinkle, Twinkle." Have children repeat the last word, *star.* Tell them to listen to the next line and raise their hands when they hear the word that rhymes with *star.* Repeat the procedure for the last two lines. Play the poem on the tape and invite children to listen and raise their hands when they hear the words that rhyme. (*star, are; high, sky*)

▶ Reread the poem "Day and Night" on pages 6 and 7. Ask children to find words that rhyme. (*sound, round*) Have children name other rhyming words. (*found, ground, hound*)

After You Read

Read or listen to the sentences.
Match each sentence with its picture.

❶		ⓐ	Hello, sun. I wonder where you are.
❷		ⓑ	The sun goes down. The moon comes up.
❸		ⓒ	The moon is high in the sky.
❹		ⓓ	The sun goes down.
❺		ⓔ	The moon sees me.
❻		ⓕ	A star is spinning.
❼		ⓖ	A diamond twinkles.
❽		ⓗ	The world is round.

9

WRITER'S CORNER

Beginning

● **To write a poem**

PRE-WRITE: Ask children to look at "I See the Moon." Provide a model for them to copy or supply the poem with blank spaces. WRITE: Encourage them to write a new poem by substituting *moon* with a word of their choice. Suggest that they may want to use one of their new vocabulary words, such as *sun, earth,* or *star.* Encourage them to write and illustrate their new poems. PUBLISH: Bind the poems created by children of all three levels into a book for all to enjoy.

Intermediate

● **To write a shape poem**

PRE-WRITE: Draw one large circle and one smaller circle on the chalkboard. Label the large one *sun* and the smaller one *moon.* Brainstorm with children what they know and think about the sun and moon. List their responses in the appropriate circles. WRITE: As a group, compose a "shape poem" by writing words around the perimeter of a circle. Then provide each child with a paper circle. Help them select words from the brainstorming list to use in their own shape poem about the moon or the sun. Have students write their poems around their paper circles. PUBLISH: Invite children to decorate and color their poems to look more like the sun or moon and add them to the class book.

Advanced

● **To write a shape poem**

PRE-WRITE: Have small groups of students work together to tell what words they think describe the sun, moon, Earth, and stars. Label each of four sheets of chart paper *sun, moon, Earth,* and *stars.* Then record (or have a volunteer record) on the appropriate chart the suggested words for each heavenly body. WRITE: Invite each child to choose one heavenly body and draw its shape on construction paper. Then have students use the suggested words, other ideas, and words in their home languages to create a shape poem. REVISE, EDIT: Help children suggest additions and changes to each other's poems. PUBLISH: Add the poems to the class book.

For coordinating activities, see the CD-ROM disk that corresponds with this theme.

What Do Children Know?

On chart paper, create a word web in the shape of the sun and label it "The Sun." On the rays, record what children already know. To assess their knowledge, ask questions such as:

▶ *Where is the sun? Point to it.* **(P)***

▶ *Is the sun round or square?* **(EP)***

▶ *When do you see the sun?* **(SE)***

▶ *What is the sun like?* **(NF)***

What Do Children Want to Know?

Model, then read chorally, the words on the web. Then ask what children would like to find out about the sun and record their questions on a separate sheet of chart paper. Accept home-language responses, translating them (with other children's help) and adding these ideas to the chart. Have children pronounce the words. Encourage children to add words or pictures to the web as they study the sun.

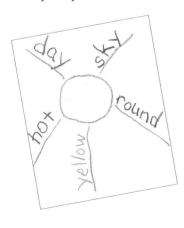

Theme Presentation

OBJECTIVES

● READING To assess prior knowledge

● LISTENING/SPEAKING To act out a song/ To comprehend language used in context

KEY VOCABULARY

cold, heat, hot, light, sunshine, warm

Introduce

▶ To introduce children to their friend the sun, you may wish to darken the classroom, project Transparency 3, and play "Mister Sun" (from *Singable Songs for the Very Young* by Raffi) or another song.

▶ As you replay the sun song, ask children to join you in creating movements. *(Make a round sun with your arms; move like the sun in the sky.)* Create other movements for the words in the song.

▶ Ask children to look at the pictures on page 10. Explain that the pictures show how the sun helps us. Ask children what they see. Facilitate additional responses by focusing on one picture at a time. For example, ask children to look at the picture with the cat and ask:

Where is the sun? Show me. **(P)***
Is it day or night in the picture? **(EP)***
What is making the icicles melt? **(SE)***
Why do you think the cat is sitting in front of the window? **(NF)***

Practice

Invite children to work on Activity Page 3. Some less fluent students may benefit by first pointing and talking about who and what goes in each box. After the page is completed, invite children to sit in a circle to tell each other about their pictures.

Evaluate

You may create a listening activity to evaluate children's comprehension. Take on the persona of the sun, weaving in as many of the vocabulary words as possible. *Example: I am a big, beautiful star. I see my friends* [supply children's names]. *I see the girls/boys* [supply names]. *I warm the earth. I give light. I help the flowers/trees/grass grow.* (Continue telling the sun's story.) *Who am I?*

Observe students' reactions to judge informally their level of comprehension and their ability to understand some unfamiliar vocabulary when used in context.

Preview • *Our Friend the Sun*

Vocabulary Preview

▶ Children at this age love to hear their names, so adapt the poem "I See the Moon" on page 4 by substituting each student's name for the word *moon*. For example: *I see Juan, and Juan sees me . . .* Then substitute the word *sun* or *star* and invite children to join in. Encourage children to use the pictures on Transparency 4 or pages 10 and 11 to help them suggest other words they might substitute for the word *moon*.

▶ Ask children to look at the first picture on page 11. Encourage them to talk about what they see. Explain that most flowers start out as seeds and then, with the help of the sun, pop through the earth, grow, and eventually bloom into beautiful flowers. Invite children to crouch down and pretend they are flower seeds planted deep in the ground. Play a song about the sun as you move about the room "watering" the seeds. Encourage children to "grow" and "bloom" into beautiful flowers.

▶ Draw children's attention to the second picture on page 11. Encourage them to name the objects they see. Then use the words *tree, grass,* and *butterfly* as you tell a story about the picture. Have interested students tell their own stories about the picture. Continue in a similar manner as you discuss the last picture, using the words *girl, boy,* and *friend*.

Looking Ahead

Have children find and read the title of the selection. Discuss the purpose of the title. Then invite children to look at the pictures in the selection and predict the ways the sun is a friend to the earth.

*Language Acquisition Levels: P = PREPRODUCTION; EP = EARLY PRODUCTION; SE = SPEECH EMERGENCE; NF = NEARLY-FLUENT

Rereading for Different Purposes

▶ On a second reading you might choose to echo-read the selection. Read a phrase or sentence while the children track or point to each word as it's read. After you complete the sentence or phrase, have children "echo," that is, repeat what's been read.

▶ While using the audio tape, have students read the story again to see how many different animals they can find and name.

Reading the Literature

Our Friend the Sun

Introduce

▶ Provide magazine pictures of people, animals, plant life, and food. (*Natural History, National Geographic*, gardening magazines, and the newspaper food sections are good sources.) Ask children to collect pictures of things that need the sun. Invite them to use the pictures to make a large collage. Have children add to the collage whenever they think or learn about another thing that needs the sun. You may use the collage to check vocabulary and comprehension after reading the selection.

▶ If the weather is right, you might choose to begin this reading outdoors so everyone can experience the warmth of their friend the sun. Have children stand in the shade for a few minutes and then in the sun. Encourage them to tell how they felt in both locations and why they felt that way.

Read

▶ You may wish to have children sit in a reading circle with Transparency 3 displayed in the background. Invite children to imagine and enjoy the "warmth and sunlight" as you read the selection.

▶ As you read each page, have children point to the corresponding illustration as each thing is mentioned. Allow them to help each other.

On This Page

▶ Tell children that a *friend* is someone who knows you, likes you, and helps you. If possible, show children a picture of you and a friend having fun. Tell children about your friend. Invite children to name one of their friends and to tell what they like to do together.

▶ Verify that children understand the meaning of *guess. (to give an answer even if you aren't sure)*

Language Focus

- **Descriptive adjectives**
- *Have/has*

▶ After students have read and enjoyed the entire selection, use crayons or markers to draw a picture of a colorful flower and another picture of a brown, wilted flower. Ask children to point to the pretty flower. Ask children which word helped them decide what flower to point to. *(pretty)* Tell children that the word *pretty* describes the flower. Ask what the opposite of *pretty* is. *(ugly)*

▶ Challenge children to use adjectives to describe the things pictured in the

LITERATURE
PART
2
NONFICTION

Our Friend the Sun
Written by Janet Palazzo

This pretty flower has a friend.
This little butterfly has a friend.
These girls and boys have a friend.
Who is their friend?
Can you guess?

12   Sun, Moon, Earth, Stars

story. For example: *big tree, tall grass, little butterfly, clear sky,* and *big sun.*

▶ Reread the selection, emphasizing the words *has* and *have.* Explain that *has* and *have* mean the same thing. *Has* is used with one thing: *The flower* (one flower) *has a friend. Have* is used with two or more: *The girls and boys have a friend.* Mention other items (*trees, butterfly, grass, boy*) and ask children to choose either *have* or *has.* You may wish to extend the lesson to *grow/grows.*

Meeting Individual Needs

REINFORCEMENT

▶ Doing experiments will help *logical/mathematical* learners better understand the working of the sun. Have children place a pan of ice cubes in direct sunlight and another pan of ice cubes in the shade. Invite children to see which ice cubes melt first. Encourage them to tell why they melted faster. Utilize vocabulary: *heat, hot, cold, warm.*

▶ You may wish to have children create a solar "stove." Provide children with a cut-off milk carton lined with aluminum foil. Ask children to place a small piece of cheese on a corn chip, cover it with plastic wrap, and put it into the solar stove. Have children set the stoves in direct sunlight and watch to see how long it takes to make solar nachos.

▶ Encourage *independent* learners to choose new words learned during the reading. Ask them to write each word on an index card. Suggest that they use these word cards to help them retell the story. Some children may be able to use the cards to write some of the main ideas of the story. Encourage them to illustrate their work.

BUILDING SELF-ESTEEM

Ask children how sunshine makes them feel. Confirm that sunshine often makes people feel good or happy. Invite children to sit in a circle (in the sun, if possible). Encourage them to tell what happened in the last few days that made them feel good. This could be something they saw, something they did, or something nice that someone said to them.

You may wish to schedule regular meetings in the "sunshine circle" to acknowledge children's achievements.

CHALLENGE

Encourage more fluent children to create riddles about the sun's friends from the story and the art. Be sure to model the activity first. *Example: I grow green on the ground. What am I? I purr when I sleep in the sun. What am I?* Encourage children to refer to their books and classroom displays for ideas. You may want to have children put their riddles in a book to share with others.

This is their friend— the sun.

13

Cross-Curricular Connections

SCIENCE

▶ Invite children to create a classroom window garden. You will need some potting soil; fast-growing seeds, such as hardy daisies, beans, or lettuce; and plant containers. Explain how water and light from the sun help things grow. You might also organize a watering schedule and invite volunteers to care for the garden.

▶ Invite children to make sundials. You will need empty coffee cans, sand, and sticks. Help children fill the cans with sand and place a stick in the center. Place sundials in a sunny spot and have children observe throughout the day the length and location of the stick's shadow. Invite children to tell how the shadow changed.

▶ Display a large classroom calendar. Review or introduce the days of the week. Provide children with key weather symbols: small pictures of an umbrella, a sun, a cloud, and a snowflake. Have them record their observations by writing the appropriate symbol in the calendar box each day.

HEALTH

Ask children if there are times when the sun can be bad for you. If necessary, add that skin (especially fair skin) can be burned by the sun. Too much heat from the sun can make you sick. Looking directly at the sun can hurt your eyes. Invite students to suggest ways to protect themselves, for example, using sunglasses, an umbrella, long-sleeved shirt, hat, and sunscreen. You might bring in these items for children to tell how they are used. Groups of students could prepare a book on "sun safety."

SOCIAL STUDIES/MULTICULTURAL

Exhibit pictures of other cultures that show housing, clothing, and environment. Facilitate discussion of how homes and clothing are designed to protect people from the heat or cold. For example, in northern climates architects often design buildings with many windows on the south side to let in all available sunlight and warmth.

Mainstream Connections

Encourage children to invite their mainstream classmates to see their window gardens and sundials.

On This Page

Help children understand that we all live on the planet Earth. Set out the globe and help children locate their families' home countries. Point out where they live now. Tell children that the globe is a model of the earth.

Language Focus

● **Opposites**

▶ Tell children that opposites are as different from each other as can be. For example: *up/down, day/night, high/low.* Encourage children to suggest opposites for the words *pretty* (*ugly*) and *little* (*big*).

▶ Ask children to look through the story and find words that name opposites. (*far, close; cold, hot*) Write these words in a two-column chart. You may also include words from Part 1. (*dark/light*) Then encourage children to suggest other opposites to add to the chart. Looking through magazines may give them ideas.

Sunshine helps the flowers bloom.
Sunshine helps the grass grow tall.
Sun makes the earth a home for us all.

Everyday Talk

- **Describing weather conditions**
- **Describing physical reactions and feelings**

Review with children common expressions used to talk about the weather. *(It is warm/ cold out. It's rainy/sunny/windy/cloudy. It's snowing/raining.)* Invite children to use these expressions to talk about the weather.

When children are comfortable talking about the weather, write the following sentence starter on the board: *When it's rainy out, I am___.* Encourage children to tell how they react to the temperature or how the weather makes them feel: *cold, warm, wet, sad.* Continue by giving sentence starters.

The sun is a star.
It is our special star.

The sun is a big and fiery ball.
It is far away from us—
　　　　but not *too* far!

If the sun was too far,
we'd be too cold.
If the sun was too close,
we'd be too hot.

15

Theme Project Update

✎ As children finish reading and talking about *Our Friend the Sun,* encourage them to think of how they might use what they learned for their museum. Ideas include:

▶ Make a snack to serve the guests who visit the science museum. Children might want to make sun tea.

▶ Have children create posters to advertise the science museum. Encourage them to use some of the project ideas on their posters.

▶ Make exhibits about the negative effects of the sun and how to avoid them or protect yourself from them.

▶ Make sunshine name tags to wear when the science museum is open to visitors.

　▶ Create models of how the sun helps its friends. Using buttons, chenille stems, small stones, scraps of fabric, construction paper, and other craft supplies, children can make butterflies, birds, girls, boys, trees, and flowers.

On This Page

▶ Have children tell why they think the sun is a special star. Help them understand that the sun is special because it does things for us that the other stars do not do, for example, gives us light and heat.

▶ To have children experience heat and light from near and far, place a lighted 60-watt bulb in the center of a darkened room. Taking appropriate safety measures, have children experience the heat and light from near and then from far. Lead them to conclude that the heat of the bulb decreases as you move farther away, and the light becomes less strong. Compare the light bulb to the sun. Help children understand that we feel the heat and see the light of the sun because it is closer to Earth than the other stars.

What Did Children Learn?

Ask children to look at the word web and question sheet they created before reading the story. Read the questions aloud and have children answer them, if they can. Encourage children to use the words on the word web to help them write a class story about the sun.

WRITER'S JOURNAL

Invite children to write about how the sun makes them feel. They may write about or draw a portrait of themselves doing something in the sun that they enjoy.

HOME–SCHOOL CONNECTION

Invite students to take home *Sun, Moon, Earth, Stars* or help them select library books to take home. Encourage them to read and discuss the material with family members.

After You Read

Post-Reading Activities

> **OBJECTIVES**
>
> ● **READING** To draw conclusions/To note details
> ● **LISTENING/SPEAKING** To follow directions/To role-play/To listen for specific details/To retell a story

Vocabulary Check

▶ Write the words *girls, boys, butterfly, cold, hot, far, close, sunshine, light, star, friend, flowers, grass, trees,* and *warm* on yellow construction-paper circles. Place the words in a container or paper bag. Invite children to pick out a word and, if possible, read it aloud. (You may wish to read the words for the less fluent students.) Encourage each child to draw a picture on the board or pantomime the meaning of the chosen word. For example, a student may ask two girls to stand together to show the meaning of *girls,* or a student may stand up and shiver to demonstrate *cold.* More fluent students may use these words to discuss what they have learned about the sun.

▶ Invite children to look at the collage they made before reading the selection. Encourage them to use their new vocabulary as they talk about why the objects pictured on the collage need the sun.

Comprehension Check

▣ Ask children to look at the pictures at the top of page 17. Invite a volunteer to read the directions aloud. Then divide the children into small groups and encourage them to compare and contrast the two scenes. When the groups are finished, bring all the children back together to discuss their findings.

Practice

▶ Children might practice using descriptive adjectives by looking at pages 10 and 11 and describing what they see in the pictures.

▶ Story Card 3 provides children with an opportunity to talk about how important the sun is. This card will help them visualize that the sun is needed to grow the food we need to live.

Looking Back at the Story

▶ Have children look through *Our Friend the Sun* to act out what the following friends of the sun do on a sunny day: butterflies, girls and boys, flowers, birds. After the pantomiming, have children tell about their actions.

▶ Invite students to think about how the sun is like a friend. Then ask in which ways the sun can be harmful. *(It can give you a sunburn, hurt your eyes, or make the land too dry.)* Ask questions such as: *Can a friend hurt you? Can a friend be far away?*

> **On This Page**

Verify that children understand the meaning of *enough. (not too much, not too little)* The Everyday Talk section on page 17 may help them.

Evaluate

▶ Display Transparency 4 and encourage children to tell a story about each picture. Encourage children to include the sun in each of the stories. Use this activity to judge the students' progress since beginning Part 2, as well as since the beginning of the theme.

▶ Explain that a portfolio is a good way to keep track of progress over time and that you and they will choose samples of their work to include in their portfolios. Samples may include written work or oral work recorded on an audio cassette. It might even include a video!

But our special star is just far enough.
It's just far enough
to help things grow—
like animals, flowers and trees,
and you and me!

16 Sun, Moon, Earth, Stars

Everyday Talk

● **Complaining**
● **Describing extremes**

▶ Encourage children to look at the cartoon at the bottom of page 17. Invite children to talk about what is happening. Ask volunteers to read the cartoon aloud. Have children practice these phrases as they pretend they are placing a foot into a tub of water or responding to the complaint.

▶ Read or tell the story "Goldilocks and the Three Bears." Encourage children to listen to the sentences that describe extremes of things in the story. *(This is too hot/cold/small/big/hard/soft!*

and finally the "happy medium," *This is just right!)*

◪ Have children brainstorm situations in which they and others complain. Then invite them to role-play the situations in small groups. Ask volunteers to present their role-playing to the rest of the class.

For coordinating activities, see the CD-ROM disk that corresponds with this theme.

WRITER'S CORNER

Have students at all levels work on invitations to their science museum.

Beginning

● **To draw illustrations for an invitation**
● **To copy words**

PRE-WRITE: Talk about the different things that will be exhibited at the science museum. Encourage children to walk around and see the activities students are working on. WRITE: Invite children to illustrate the invitations to the science museum. Encourage them to include drawings of some of the things that guests will see at the museum. Write the words *You Are Invited* on the board. Ask children to copy these words on the invitations. REVISE, EDIT: Invite children to share their drawings and ask for suggestions. Have them revise their work as they wish. PUBLISH: Save the invitations for the more advanced students to complete.

Intermediate and Advanced

● **To write an invitation**

PRE-WRITE: Display several commercial invitations for children to examine. Encourage intermediate and advanced students to work together to plan the information they would like to include in their invitations. Suggest that they write at least one sentence to tell the guests what they will see at the museum. WRITE: Encourage advanced students to write the information on scrap paper. REVISE, EDIT: Ask students to share their information with classmates and revise as needed. When the revisions are made, have the intermediate students copy the information onto the invitations that were illustrated by the beginning students. PUBLISH: Send the invitations to the guests.

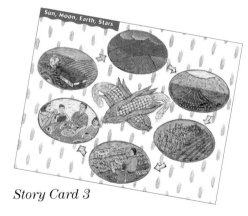

Story Card 3

After You Read

Look at the pictures.
How are they the same? How are they different?

EVERYDAY TALK

•Complaining
•Describing extremes

IT'S TOO HOT!

IT'S TOO COLD!

IT'S JUST RIGHT!

YOU ARE TOO FUSSY!

Roger Raccoon is complaining about something. What does he say? What does his mom say?

17

Out in Space

READING STRATEGIES / CRITICAL THINKING SKILLS

- Comparing and contrasting
- Noting details
- Observing

OBJECTIVES

- **READING** To recognize captions/To interpret a graphic device
- **LISTENING/SPEAKING** To tell a story/ To role-play emergency situations

KEY VOCABULARY

space, planet, planetarium, solar system, step, leap, giant, mankind, spacecraft, to land, to lift off, parade

See the Planets

Pre-Reading Tell children that some of the things they want or need to read in real life may be difficult. However, it is not necessary to understand everything or know all the words to get the information they need. The Just for Fun pages will help them develop strategies and become more confident about their ability to read the material in their surroundings. Do not aim for or expect them to understand everything.

▶ Set the stage by playing the theme music from *Star Trek* or *2001: A Space Odyssey*. Engage children by asking what they might see in space. Encourage them to answer the question by naming the celestial bodies they learned about in Parts 1 and 2. List their responses on the board or on chart paper.

▶ Talk about places where children can explore space, such as a planetarium or children's museum in your area. Volunteers may wish to talk about their experiences in those places.

Reading As you read the questions and multiple choice answers aloud, encourage children to think about how they would respond. Then reread the questions and have children respond by raising their hands when they hear the answer they feel is correct. Talk about their responses and help the children who chose the wrong answers understand why their answers are incorrect.

▶ Have children look at the chart and count the planets. You may want to use ordinal numbers (*first, second*) and superlatives (*closest, farthest, smallest*) in your discussion.

Point to the earth. **(P)***
Which is the smallest planet?
Which is the biggest one?
Show me. **(EP)***
Do you think that Pluto is hot or cold? Why? **(SE)***
Which do you think was the first planet people discovered? The last? Why? **(NF)***

Post-Reading Invite children to make a poster of a planetarium or the solar system. You may wish to provide circle and star patterns in various sizes. When children are finished drawing, encourage them to label the objects in their poster and give it a title. Invite beginning students to dictate their labels and titles for you to record.

*Language Acquisition Levels: P = PREPRODUCTION; EP = EARLY PRODUCTION; SE = SPEECH EMERGENCE; NF = NEARLY-FLUENT

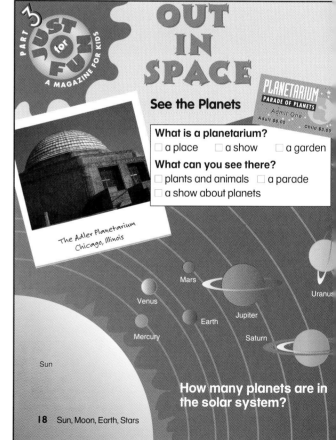

Moon Walk

Pre-Reading Prepare children for a fanciful trip through space by showing a documentary or video clips of NASA liftoffs, space travel, or conversations with astronauts in space. You might play appropriate traveling music from a New Age audio tape. Then invite children to join you in a creative movement space trip. As you verbally guide them, demonstrate through movement the words *lift-off* and *land;* the direction words (*right, left, up, down*); and other vocabulary as you make your journey.

Reading Direct children's attention to the newspaper article. Invite them to tell what they think is happening in the photo. Then encourage volunteers to locate and read the name of the newspaper, the date, and the title of the article. Finally, read the beginning of the article and the photo caption aloud. Encourage children to comment on this newspaper clipping or share any information they can about space exploration.

▶ Check for basic understanding, using questions and statements such as the following:

Show me an astronaut. **(P)***
Is the spacecraft on the moon or on Earth? **(EP)***
When did the men land on the moon? **(SE)***
What do you think about what Neil Armstrong said? **(NF)***

You may wish to explain that *mankind* means "all people on Earth."

▶ Ask children to look at the two photos at the top of page 19 as you read the captions aloud. Then have a volunteer read the questions aloud and encourage children to share their answers.

Post-Reading Invite children to make their own illustrated stories about space. Distribute Activity Page 4 and read the directions aloud. Encourage invented spelling, home-language labels, or dictation from less fluent children. Offer to assist those who wish help in labeling, dictating, or writing. Help children to "read" each other's stories. Display their finished stories in class.

Pluto

Neptune

Liftoff of Apollo II.

The Eagle is a smaller spacecraft than Apollo II. It landed on the moon.

Moon Walk

Would you like to go to the moon? Why or why not?

City Edition

Vol XII...No.3,456

The Daily Sun

15 CENTS
July 21, 1969

MAN ON THE MOON

HOUSTON, Monday, July 21—Yesterday two American astronauts landed on the moon. Millions of people watched on TV.

"That's one small step for man, one giant leap for mankind," declared Neil A. Armstrong, the first person to walk on the moon.

19

Everyday Talk

- Calling for and getting help
- Handling emergency situations

▶ You may wish to create a sense of anticipation about the cartoon feature on page 20 by wondering aloud what's happening to Scooter, Daisy, and Roger.

▶ Help children understand what is going on in the two cartoon frames. You may wish to begin by having your nearly-fluent students tell what they think is going on. Read each speech balloon and have children track the words.

▶ To check the understanding of less fluent students, use questions such as the following:

Show me Daisy. Show me Scooter. Are they on Earth? In space? (P)*

Is everything OK, or is there some trouble? What's the matter? Who will help? (EP)*

Note: The following activities need to be handled with a great deal of sensitivity because they might be traumatic for children who have gone through emergency situations or who have had problems in their neighborhoods.

▶ Discuss the importance of knowing what to say and do in an emergency. Invite children to talk about times when they might need to call for help.

Chart their responses. You may wish to have children illustrate the emergency situations on the chart in order to reinforce the concepts. Then read the expressions on page 20, and have children identify the situations they apply to. Elicit or introduce a limited number of other appropriate expressions. Practice them with the class.

▶ Have children role-play the situations described at the bottom of the page. Direct one child to play the role of someone who needs help. Have the other child be the helper. Encourage children to use the expressions on page 20 as prompts.

▶ To reinforce learning and the use of effective communication, have children role-play emergency situations with dolls or puppets.

Extension Activities

▶ Invite caregivers (such as the school nurse) or local authorities (such as a police officer, a firefighter, or the principal) to talk with children about emergencies. You may wish to talk about what to do when a child gets sick at school, when a fire breaks out, or when an earthquake or tornado occurs.

▶ Provide children with a telephone book. Show them the page or pages that list emergency phone numbers. You may wish to have children make up their own lists. Encourage children to take their lists home, add numbers of family or neighbors, and place it in a prominent place.

▶ Have children work in groups to plan and prepare a guide showing the places in the school where they can go for help. *(main office, fire alarm, security-guard station, etc.)* Challenge children to make a map that shows these places.

Here and There

Flags

Focus children's attention on the flags and invite them to describe and compare them. You may wish to display the flag page from a reference book and ask them to name other flags that show the sky, Earth, moon, or stars.

Extension Activity

Children may enjoy making their own flags that show the sun, moon, Earth, or stars. These can include flags from their home countries or original flags they create. Invite them to describe their flags and tell what they show. Display their work.

Sun Signs

Explain that the sun has always been important to people all over the world. Lead the class to discuss the sun symbols at the bottom of the page. Then present the following information:

The Aztec people of what is now called Mexico watched the sun, moon, and stars. They were able to make an accurate calendar that pointed out when to plant and harvest crops.

Native American peoples have always had a deep respect for nature and its rhythms. They honor the sun because it helps the crops grow and sets the rhythm of the seasons of the year.

Scandinavians—Danes, Norwegians, Swedes, and Finns—live in northern Europe where there is little sunlight in winter. The ancient Scandinavians respected the sun's power to bring light, warmth, and green plants back to a world that had been frozen for many months.

Extension Activity

Supply children with craft materials, including silver and gold foil, glitter, confetti, fabric scraps, construction paper, glue, crayons, and markers. Invite them to make their own sun symbols. Hang their creations so that when children look up, they can see their sun symbols.

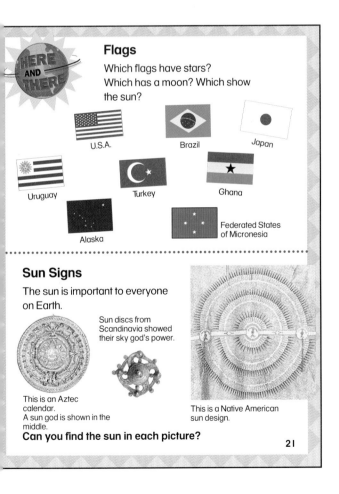

Story Card 2

Theme Project

Before children put the finishing touches on their theme projects, you may want to ask them what they enjoyed most, what was most difficult to understand, and what ideas they would like to share with others. Help individuals select some of their writings and drawings to include in their portfolios.

▶ Invite children to use the questions on page 22 as a checklist to be sure they are ready for their show. You may wish to do this page together as a class or have the children work together in small, mixed proficiency groups.

▶ You might make suggestions for rehearsing a choral reading, chant, or song from Part 1 or from the additional songs and rhymes in the Big Book, pages 13 to 16.

▶ Coordinate times for other classes and family members to visit the science museum. Select greeters, tour leaders, and translators as necessary.

Extension Activities

▶ Have children use appliance boxes, mechanical clock parts, computer boards, buttons, cardboard tubes, aluminum foil, and other materials that they have found to make a large classroom rocket ship. It can serve as a learning or reading center in the children's museum.

▶ Encourage children to make flyers or posters inviting others to see their displays. Encourage them to add important details, such as when and where the viewing will take place and what can be seen at the museum. Invite beginning students to dictate their details for you to record.

Theme Wrap-Up

Theme Activity

▶ Invite a volunteer to read the title of the first picture story and the first sentence. Encourage children to tell how to read the stories.

▶ Organize children into groups to read the page. More proficient readers will probably enjoy working alone and then getting together to read the stories to one another. Less proficient readers and nonreaders can work in groups or pairs to figure out the picture puzzle stories about the earth, sun, moon, and stars.

▶ After children have figured out the puzzle sentences and read them to one another, have them reread the stories aloud to the whole group.

Oral Review

▶ Encourage the children to read aloud by inviting them to become oral story-tellers. Have children share aloud poems or nonfiction selections of their choice. Because children's reading proficiency and fluency will vary, offer them an option to tell about or read their pieces. More proficient readers may read word for word. Students who are less proficient in reading but more fluent in speaking may prefer to tell a story. Others may need you to read aloud softly with them. You may wish to have students rehearse, using a tape recorder, before they read to the class.

▶ Story Card 4 provides another way to explore the language that students are acquiring. On the back of the card are questions and statements that can be used with students at various levels of language acquisition.

▶ *Beyond the Earth* (Set II) includes a theme poster and other materials that relate to outer space and the space walk.

Self-Assessment

First, brainstorm with children and list the things they see and do during the day and at night. Then give each child two strips of heavy paper about 2 inches wide. Each should be long enough to fit around a child's head. Punch a hole at each end. Ask children to write *Day* and draw day things on one strip and to write *Night* and draw night things on the other. Use ribbon or string to join the ends together to make the strips into two headbands. Then have children put on a *Day* or a *Night* band as they tell or listen to day or night stories. Use a camcorder or tape recorder to document children's responses.

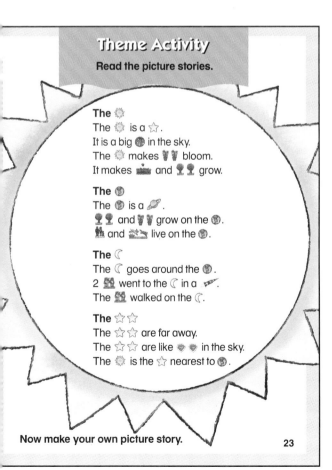

Story Card 4

Theme Bibliography

▶ Brown, Margaret Wise. *Goodnight Moon.* Harper & Row, 1947, 1975. This gentle classic shows and tells the story of a young rabbit who says good night to all the nighttime things he sees from his quiet bedroom, including the stars, the moon, and even the cow that jumps over the moon.

▶ Carle, Eric. *Papa, Please Get the Moon for Me.* Picture Book Studio, 1986. Children will enjoy reading this delightful story about a father who tries to fulfill his daughter's wish. This book can also be used to introduce the eternal cycle of the moon.

▶ Hatchett, Clint. *The Glow-in-the-Dark Night Sky Book.* Random House, 1988. This book provides both diagrams and illustrations of the more than thirty constellations that appear in the sky. The diagrams, which are painted with nontoxic ink, glow in the dark after they are exposed to light.

▶ Jeunesse, Gallimard, and Verdet, Jean-Pierre. *The Earth and Sky.* Scholastic, 1992. With the use of acetate pages, children can explore the inside of the earth, watch the earth travel around the sun, and much more.

▶ Nelson, JoAnne. *Day and Night.* McClanahan Book Company, 1990. Simple rhyming text and informative illustrations help children see what happens in the sky to turn day into night.

▶ Novak, Matt. *Claude and Sun.* Bradbury Press, 1987. This delightful story tells about a man named Claude and the wonderful time he has with the sun.

See also the Professional Bibliography in the Teacher's Companion.

PRENTICE HALL REGENTS
A VIACOM COMPANY

© 1996 by Prentice Hall Regents
Prentice Hall Inc.
A Viacom Company
Upper Saddle River, NJ 07458

Printed in the United States of America

10 9 8 7 6 5 4 3

ISBN 0-13-438730-9

Prentice-Hall International (UK) Limited, London
Prentice-Hall of Australia Pty. Limited, Sydney
Prentice-Hall Canada Inc., Toronto
Prentice-Hall Hispanoamerican, SA., Mexico
Prentice-Hall of India Private Limited, New Delhi
Prentice-Hall of Japan, Inc., Tokyo
Simon & Schuster Asia Pte. Ltd., Singapore
Editora Prentice-Hall do Brasil, Ltda., Rio de Janeiro

Prentice Hall Regents
Publisher: Marilyn Lindgren
Development Editors: Carol Callahan, Fredrik Liljeblad, Kathleen Ossip
Assistant Editor: Susan Frankle
Director of Production: Aliza Greenblatt
Manufacturing Buyer: Dave Dickey
Production Coordinator: Ken Liao
Marketing Manager: Richard Seltzer

Editorial, Design, Production and Packaging
McClanahan & Company, Inc.

Project Director: Susan Cornell Poskanzer
Creative Director: Lisa Olsson
Design Director: Toby Carson
Director of Production: Karen Pekarne

TEACHERS EDITION
Illustration: Cyd Moore, cover; Dartmouth Publishing p1
Photography: Ken Karp Photography p4, p5

STORY CARDS
Illustration: Karen Blessen SC1, Julie Durrell SC2, Joanna Roy SC3, Steve Sanford SC4

Reduced Student Book art is credited in Student Book.